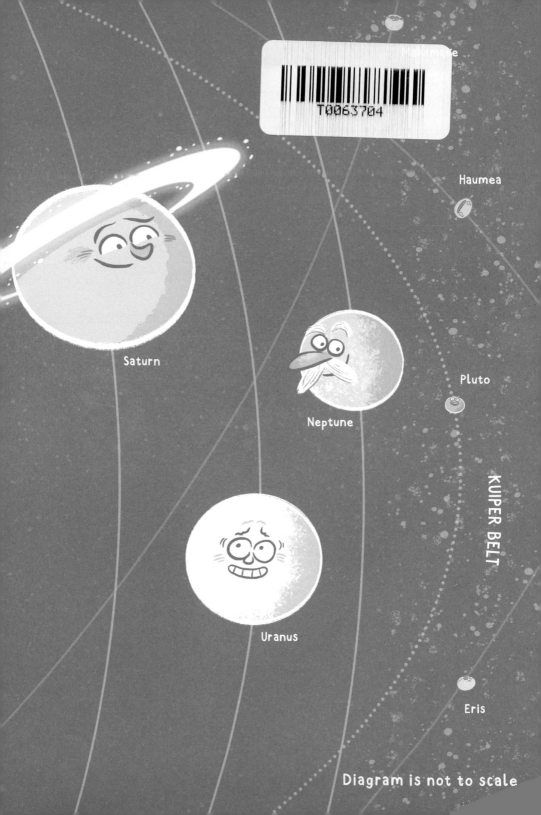

# HOW TO TEACH GROWN-UPS ABOUT PLUTO

# HOW TO TEACH GROWN-UPS ABOUT PLUTO

By **DEAN REGAS**

Illustrated by **AARON BLECHA**

**BRITANNICA BOOKS**

# Contents

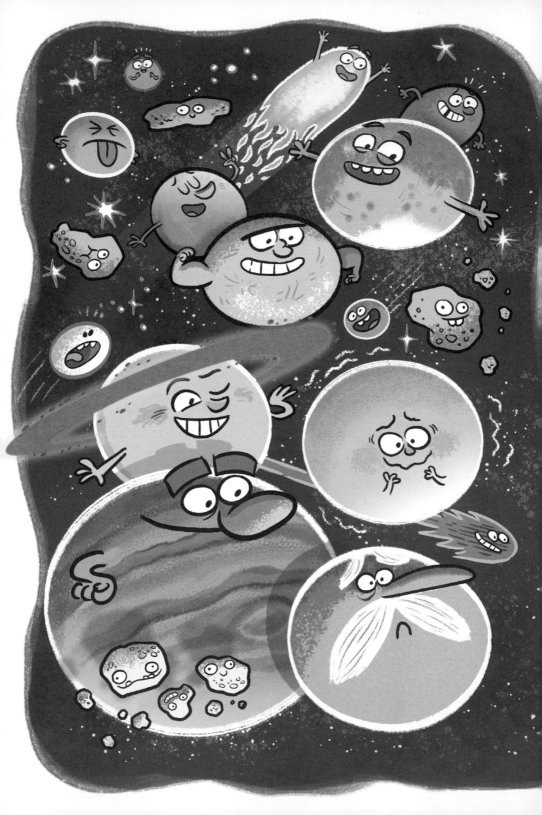

# Welcome to Space

Do your grown-ups seem to be under the illusion they're always in the right? Do they think it's always *they* who should be doing the teaching, and you who should be doing the listening? Well, it's time for a fresh approach, especially when it comes to the cutting-edge science of our solar system.

Before we begin this important education of your grown-ups, let me introduce myself. I'm Dean and I'm an astronomer. Being an astronomer is the greatest job in the universe. I study everything from the Moon to the stars, planets to galaxies, comets, and even the Sun. And by working

Astronomer
Dean Regas

at an observatory, I get to look through humongous, gigantic telescopes.

My job isn't all staying-up-all-night and sleeping-until-noon (although that is a nice perk). My main duty is to teach people about outer space and share the latest discoveries made by astronomers around the world. Each day I learn something new—and then I get to share those cool facts with others. And what I've noticed is that our ideas about space are always changing. That's what makes astronomy even more fun!

One of those changes has upset quite a lot of people.

You'll find observatories with giant telescopes around the world.

McDonald Observatory, United States

Llano de Chajnantor Observatory, Chile

Pluto's no longer a planet. You know it, I know it, and most of the astronomers around the world know it. But there are some people (mostly older people) who cling to the notion that Pluto *should* still be a planet. They remember the good old days when Pluto was a planet and there were nine planets in the solar system. Habits are hard to break, and adults' fascination with Pluto as a planet is a challenge for us. How can we help them move on and enter the 21st century?

Look, let's be honest: You know *way* more about space than grown-ups do. The last time they studied astronomy was

Royal Observatory, Greenwich, UK

South African Astronomical Observatory, South Africa

3

SUN

Venus

Mars

Earth

Mercury

like 1,000 years ago. You know, back before phones and cars were invented. Okay, maybe not *that* far back.

During their school days, they may have memorized this mnemonic device: My Very Educated Mother Just Served Us Nine Pizzas. This catchy saying helped them remember the order of the planets from the closest to the Sun to the farthest from the Sun. The first letter of each word represented the first letter of a planet: Mercury, Venus, Earth, Mars, Jupiter, Saturn, Uranus, Neptune, Pluto.

Neptune

Saturn

Pluto

Uranus

Jupiter

This is the order of planets in the solar system that your grown-ups would have learned about in school.

Now "Pizzas" is gone. Adults *love* pizzas. This was probably the high point of their school life. And to the average adult, the names of the planets are the one thing they remember from childhood—the one thing they know about the solar system. It's understandable that they want to cling to this.

But things will be okay. And it's not their fault that they are a little behind. They've been busy doing other, non-astronomy things. But I know it can be frustrating when you talk about space and all the amazing things you're learning in school about the universe, and all they can add is, "Pluto should still be a planet!"

So if you're tired of hearing adults say "Back in my day…" and you want to educate them, this book is for you. First, let's dive into a little history behind this Pluto debate so you can be more informed than your grown-ups when you tell

Back in my day…

them the truth about Pluto. We'll look at how it was found and why it is not a planet anymore. And because you will be explaining all this to your grown-ups, we had better make it very, very easy.

# Earth's a Planet?
# That's Revolutionary

First off, I have a confession. I *used* to think Pluto was a planet. I even defended Pluto's planethood to other astronomers and the public.

I know, it's embarrassing now.

It was difficult to lose a planet from my childhood. I went through the five classic stages of grief:

**1. Denial:** "Uh-uh. No way. Pluto is still a planet."

**2. Anger:** "How *dare* they do that to poor Pluto!"

**3. Bargaining:** "Okay, I'll let in some other planets *if* you keep Pluto a planet."

**4. Depression:** "It's hopeless. Pluto is not a planet and that stinks."

**5. Acceptance:** "It's okay. That's science!"

Your grown-ups may be somewhere along this path. Are they in denial? Angry? Depressed? Be prepared for them to go through these stages.

Denial

Anger

Even as an astronomer, it took me time to realize the Pluto I knew as a kid is different from the Pluto we know today. Pluto hasn't changed. But our understanding about Pluto has changed a lot!

What helped me? I first learned the history of "planets" and how we've grappled with this subject before. So that's where we're going to start with your grown-ups. Let's set the scene for them.

Bargaining Depression Acceptance

Five hundred years ago, before the invention of the telescope, people could still see a lot of stuff in the sky just by looking up. Astronomers could observe the twinkling stars that remained in fixed patterns we call constellations. There were also seven other things that they called planets.
To them, a planet was anything that moved across the stars from day to day and month to month. They didn't think of planets as round worlds of gas and rock as we do now.

To them, planets wandered around the star constellations.

In fact, the word *planet* comes from the Greek phrase *asteres planetai*, which means "wandering stars." Each night the seven planets would move just a little bit.

The seven planets in the ancient world were the Sun and Moon, Mercury, Venus, Mars, Jupiter, and Saturn. Most people didn't even consider Earth to be a planet back then! Earth was just Earth—separate from space. They thought all the other stuff in the universe circled around Earth.

Astronomers watched the planets wander for centuries. Eventually, they could predict where each planet would be decades in the future. That's some serious science!

So a planet, back then, was just a weird moving star. But a Polish astronomer named Nicolaus Copernicus changed all that. In 1503–04, he was observing Mars and Saturn and there was a problem. Neither planet was

where it was supposed to be in the sky. He consulted his old, dusty science books and saw they were wrong. Copernicus decided to fix the errors by creating a revolutionary model for the planets. He wrote something pretty shocking.

Planets don't go around Earth; they go around the Sun! That meant the Sun was *not* a planet, and Earth, the place where we live, *was* a planet. And the Moon wasn't a planet

I guess the universe DOESN'T revolve around me!

Nicolaus Copernicus

# GEOCENTRIC vs. HELIOCENTRIC
## (WHO'S IN THE MIDDLE?)

Five hundred years ago, most Europeans thought Earth stayed at the center of the solar system and the other planets moved around it in a geocentric model (geo = Earth). Then Nicolaus Copernicus put the Sun at the center of the solar system. In his heliocentric model (helio = Sun), Earth and the planets went around the Sun.

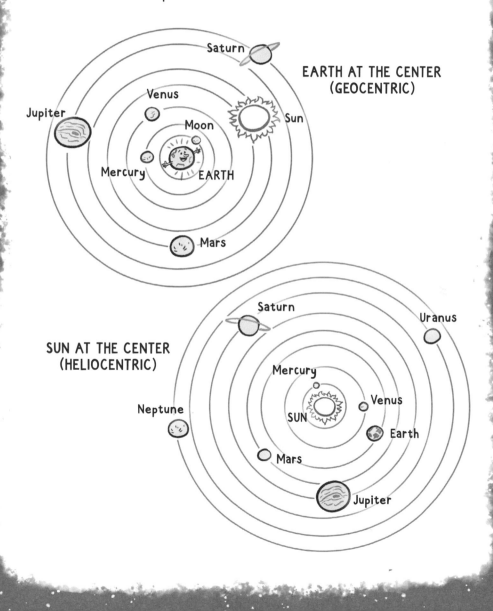

EARTH AT THE CENTER
(GEOCENTRIC)

Saturn

Venus

Jupiter

Moon

Sun

Mercury

EARTH

Mars

SUN AT THE CENTER
(HELIOCENTRIC)

Saturn

Uranus

Mercury

Venus

SUN

Neptune

Earth

Mars

Jupiter

because it went *around* a planet (Earth). Ancient astronomers from Greece, India, and the Islamic world had tried to explain this, but Copernicus was the first to calculate precisely how, and to reach a wide audience. So you might say Copernicus was the first person to officially kick planets out of the planet club. And, in a weird way, he became the first person to discover a new planet: planet Earth.

It took a long time for people to come around to the fact that Copernicus was right—like 100 years or more. But slowly people agreed that a planet was no longer a "wandering star" but instead "an object that goes around the Sun." And now there were six planets: Mercury, Venus, *Earth*, Mars, Jupiter, and Saturn.

# Where Is Uranus?

The next planet was discovered in 1781 by English astronomer William Herschel, who was often helped by his sister Caroline. He was looking through his telescope and saw a little round ball. He watched the ball for a few nights and it moved! It moved like a planet farther away than Saturn. Herschel thought it was a comet at first, but he eventually figured out it was a planet, one that we now call Uranus. Now if your grown-ups start to giggle at the mention of Uranus, please tell them to calm down. This is serious!

So Herschel added a new element to the definition of a planet. It not only was an object that went around the Sun, it also looked like a round ball when you looked at it through a telescope.

What was beyond Uranus? Astronomers really wanted to discover another new planet.

URANUS!

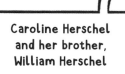

Caroline Herschel and her brother, William Herschel

# Planets Found and Kicked Out

In 1801, Italian astronomer Giuseppe Piazzi discovered a new planet. It was really small and looked like a tiny dot in his telescope, but it circled the Sun between Mars and Jupiter. Piazzi named the new planet Ceres.

In 1802, another astronomer found Pallas, another tiny planet between Mars and Jupiter. And then two more were found (named Juno and Vesta). All four new planets looked puny in a telescope, so they changed the planet definition a bit. A planet *didn't* have to be big and round. It simply had to be something that went around the Sun. So by 1807, there were 11 planets!

Astronomers kept finding more little "planets." By 1850, joining the big and round planets were 13 dinky planets: Ceres, Pallas, Juno, Vesta, Astraea, Hebe, Iris, Flora, Metis, Hygiea, Parthenope, Victoria, and Egeria.

This was getting crazy: too many planets! Astronomers decided that the definition of a planet needed to be updated again. Thirteen of the objects were just too small. Astronomers agreed a planet had to be, once more, a *big* and round thing that went around the Sun. The former dinky planets were given a new category: asteroids. Asteroids are small objects of rock and metal that mainly circle the Sun between Mars and Jupiter. Astronomers have now found more than 1,000,000 asteroids in the solar system.

And that's the story of how 13 planets were found and then kicked out of the planet club. If your grown-ups are still upset about Pluto, casually ask them, "Why aren't you still mad about what they did to Ceres and Vesta and Pallas and Juno and Astraea and Hebe...?"

Aha, now you've stumped them!

# Finding a Planet Without Even Looking

In the 1840s, two mathematicians named Urbain Le Verrier and John Couch Adams were studying how Uranus moved and thought it was moving in a funny way. Now, they were in different countries and not talking to each other. But they were working on the same problem at the same time. And they came up with the same solution: There is another planet out there that no one has seen. The gravity of a mystery planet is moving Uranus around.

Le Verrier did the math and wrote to the Berlin Observatory. He said, "Point your telescope at this place in the sky and you should find a planet." Le Verrier never looked through a telescope: He was so confident that his math was right, he didn't need one. The astronomer at the Berlin Observatory, Johann Galle, read the letter and thought, Oh what the heck, I'll aim my telescope there. And sure enough, when he put his eye to the telescope, there it was: a new round planet that went around the Sun! That was how Neptune was discovered: math.

# Search for Planet X

I would absolutely love to discover a planet! How cool would that be? The people who discovered Neptune became heroes (well, scientific heroes), and other astronomers dreamed of finding another world that was even farther from the Sun. Planet hunters often called this undiscovered thing "Planet X." The hunt for Planet X became the obsession of Percival Lowell, founder of the Lowell Observatory in Flagstaff, Arizona. His plan: Point his giant telescopes and scan the sky one section at a

Pluto Discovery Dome at the Lowell Observatory in Flagstaff, Arizona

time—and eventually
Planet X would appear.
Lowell continued searching,
but upon his death in 1916,
there was still no trace of
Planet X.

The search was picked up by
a young astronomer named Clyde
Tombaugh, who carefully
photographed and rephotographed
entire sections of the sky through a special
telescope. Night after night, he looked at stars. So many
stars. So many nights! He looked for anything that moved slowly
across the background stars over time—that's what planets do.
Planet X, if it existed, would have been so far away and slow
moving that Tombaugh could not discover it in one night.
It would take weeks or months to notice it change position.

During his 14-year study, Tombaugh spent up to 7,000
hours looking at around 44,675,000 stars in his photographs.
Along the way, he discovered tons of new stars and 775 asteroids.
But he is most remembered for that fateful day in 1930, when he
first spied Pluto.

Tombaugh put two pictures into his blink comparator, a
machine that could display two images of the same section of

the sky taken days apart. By turning a dial, Tombaugh could flip between the two images. All the stars would be in the same place in both pictures. But a planet would shift position from picture to picture.

"Wait, look at that." A speck in one picture, hardly noticeable, fainter than most stars, was in a *slightly different place on the other picture*. It wandered at just the right speed to be an object beyond the orbit of Neptune. There it was. Planet X!

# PLUTO FOUND IN PICTURES

Clyde Tombaugh found Pluto by looking at pictures of the sky. Although stars stayed in the same place each night, Pluto moved. Look how tiny it is. How did he ever see it?

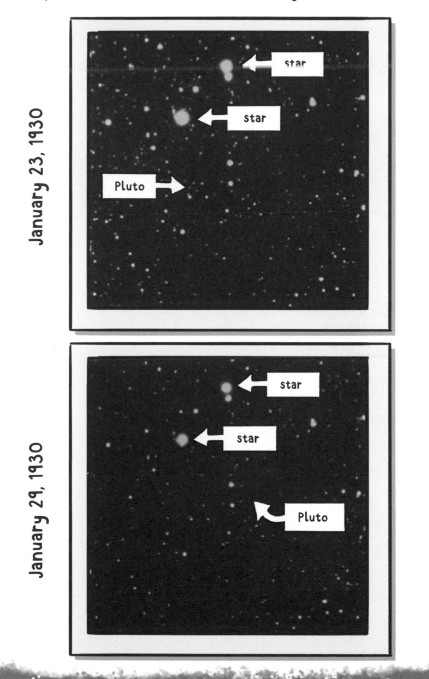

January 23, 1930

star

star

Pluto

January 29, 1930

star

star

Pluto

Tombaugh wrote about the discovery: "For the next 45 minutes or so, I was in the most excited state of mind in my life." It was really faint, but it went around the Sun so it was a new planet. Planet X was found at last!

Tombaugh became famous throughout the world. He was the discoverer of a planet that was over three billion miles (4.8 billion km) from Earth. He brought fame to the Lowell Observatory in Flagstaff, Arizona, and inspired a generation to look to the skies.

I'm still amazed by Tombaugh's discovery of Pluto. I've looked for Pluto through the biggest telescopes at my observatory, using star charts to tell me exactly where to aim, and I still haven't been able to find it! Pluto is really, really hard to see.

# How Planet X Got
# Its Name

Venetia Burney, an 11-year-old girl in England, was sitting at the breakfast table when her grandfather read about the new planet in the newspaper. He said, "I wonder what they would name it?" Venetia blurted out, "Why not call it Pluto?"

Venetia recalled a lot about that day in 1930. "I was quite interested in Greek and Roman legends at the time," she said in an interview in 2006. "At school, we used to play games in

the university park, putting—I think they were lumps of clay—at the right distance from each other to represent the distances of the planets from the Sun." From reading about the planets in books, Venetia knew that they had names from Roman mythology. Pluto was a Roman god of the underworld and because Pluto was so far from the Sun and so dark, it fit.

Venetia Burney

Pluto, Roman god of the underworld

Her grand-father thought Venetia's suggestion was so brilliant that he told an astronomer friend who, in turn, contacted the Lowell Observatory. Clyde Tombaugh thought it was perfect too. He especially liked that the first two letters, *P-L*, could pay tribute to the founder of the observatory and the original Pluto hunter, Percival Lowell. And that's how an 11-year-old girl named a new planet.

# Pluto the Shrinking Planet

So up until now, your grown-ups will probably be pretty happy with this story. You might want to sit them down at this point. Because it turns out Pluto was full of surprises.

It should have appeared round in a telescope just like Uranus and Neptune. It didn't. It looked like a faint dot—just like how every star looks in a telescope. That's okay, astronomers thought. No big deal. Pluto was *really* far away. It was still probably really big, and probably round, right?

In the beginning, Pluto seemed big because it was fairly bright. It was so bright that astronomers assumed that Pluto was as large as Earth. If it was that big and it went around the Sun, there was no doubt it was a planet.

Upon further examination, some astronomers changed their minds about Pluto's size. Their measurements showed it

I thought it would be bigger.

Pluto: shiny but tiny

to be more like the size of Mars. But Mars was definitely a planet, so Pluto was still okay.

It wasn't until 1976 that astronomers Dale Cruikshank, Carl Pilcher, and David Morrison figured out that Pluto's icy surface made it shiny like a mirror. It wasn't bright because it was big. It was bright because it was really shiny. Pluto turned out to be less than $\frac{1}{20}$ the size of Mars. The longer they looked at Pluto, the smaller it seemed to get. If this continued, astronomers joked, Pluto would soon disappear altogether!

After astronomers discovered Pluto's largest moon, called Charon, in 1978, it helped them measure the true size of Pluto. It turned out you could fit 170 Plutos inside Earth. "Hold up," some astronomers said. "Is that dinky thing really a planet?" After this discovery, astronomer Brian Marsden, associate director at the Harvard-Smithsonian Center for Astrophysics and someone who knew the most about small objects in the solar system, began considering Pluto to be more of a minor object than a planet.

# Pluto the Eccentric Planet

When your grown-ups were kids, everyone did in fact realize that not only was Pluto undersized, it also had by far the weirdest orbit of any planet. An orbit is the path each object takes around the Sun. Although orbits look like perfect circles when you look

I'm eccentric!

at them on charts, they are actually more like ovals. This shape is called an ellipse. Earth's orbit is just a little elliptical because we get only a tiny bit closer to the Sun at one point of the year and only a little farther from the Sun at another time of year. Venus's orbit is the most circular (or least elliptical), while Mercury's is significantly more oval-shaped or more elliptical.

But Pluto's orbit is waaaaay more elliptical than even Mercury's. Its path around the Sun is a long, stretched-out ellipse. Pluto even dips closer to the Sun than Neptune for 20 years and then jets out almost twice as far. Also, its orbit is slanted compared with the other planets' orbits. So although the other eight planets circle the Sun at almost the same angle, Pluto's orbit is tilted more than twice as much as any other planet.

Why is Pluto so weird? Astronomers figured out that Neptune, the much larger and more massive planet, pushed its weight around in the outer solar system. So it was Neptune that set Pluto on this strange journey. Neptune is the mover; Pluto was moved.

**FAST FACT**

Although it would be really cool if they did, Neptune and Pluto will never run into each other.

# Pluto's Long-lost Brothers and Sisters

The more astronomers learned about Pluto, the more questions it posed. Things were starting to add up: Pluto was tiny, Pluto had a weird orbit, Pluto was made of ice. Pluto was definitely an oddball!

But Pluto had three things going for it: It went around the Sun like a planet, it was round, and most of all, Pluto was incredibly popular. I mean, there is a Disney character named Pluto!

Astronomy had never seen anything like Pluto. It became a rock star (ahem, note: Pluto is neither a rock nor a star). Pluto was so small, so far away, so alone, so off-kilter, and so cold. I think people liked it because it was strange and mysterious. And people rallied to defend Pluto against anyone who wanted to take away its planethood.

Never before had the public embraced such an inanimate space object as their underdog.

And back then, even astronomers had to agree: There was no reason to change anything. Pluto was the only thing beyond Neptune. It went around the Sun and was round. That was good enough to be a planet back then. But was Pluto the final planet out there?

Astronomers found that Pluto was *not* alone in the far reaches of the solar system. In 1992, David Jewitt and Jane Luu discovered QB$_1$, a small object with a similar orbit to Pluto's. For 62 years, astronomers had thought Pluto was one of a kind, but now they found it had a sister object.

After he helped discover QB₁, Jewitt said it was "like waking up one morning and finding that your house is 10 times as big as you thought it was." Astronomers just learned there is so much more out there to find! And it turned out that Pluto is part of a whole neighborhood of Pluto-like objects.

Suddenly it became really cool for astronomers to search the outer solar system looking for more Pluto-like objects.

# Pluto's Siblings: Not Planets

So who else lives in Pluto's neighborhood? Telescopes and cameras became so advanced that they found dozens of Pluto's siblings far from the Sun. Today, there are more than 2,000 known objects in Pluto's neighborhood and we know that Pluto has a lot of company.

Pluto circles the Sun in the Kuiper Belt, a huge region of the solar system with lots of objects between three and five billion miles (between 4.8 and 8 billion km) from the Sun. Things astronomers find out there are called Kuiper Belt objects (KBOs). This is the neighborhood where Pluto lives.

The Kuiper Belt is filled with icy leftover bits of the solar system that never formed into planets. If you squished all the KBOs together like Play-Doh, they would make a ball only about 10 percent the size of Earth. Once the new KBO discoveries started adding up, suddenly astronomers weren't sure about Pluto. Some wondered, Is Pluto still planet-y enough? While others rushed to defend Pluto by saying, "So what if there are other things out by Pluto? It's still the biggest thing way out there." One astronomer even said, "Unless you find something bigger, Pluto is still a planet!"

Enter Mike Brown. An astronomer at the California Institute of Technology, he wanted to add to our understanding of the solar system. In the 2000s, he and his team discovered dozens of objects in the Kuiper Belt using a powerful new camera on a giant telescope. They found things in the distant solar system such as Makemake, a ball of ice so shiny that it reflects most of the weak sunlight that reaches it, and Haumea, an egg-shaped world circled by two tiny moons. These objects are almost as big as Pluto.

January 5, 2005, was the day Brown and his team spotted something huge. "I knew it within 60 seconds," Brown said. Years of

Eris
(the goddess of chaos)

work, mounds of data, and finally Brown had found an object equal in size to Pluto. Brown felt a little like Clyde Tombaugh on the day when he found Pluto.

Brown considered lots of different names for his newfound object but finally settled on Eris. Eris was the goddess of discord (or chaos) from ancient Greek mythology.

Eris definitely brought discord. The discovery of this "big" thing led astronomers into heated arguments. If Pluto was a planet, was Eris a planet too? What about the other things out there in Pluto's neighborhood that are almost as large? How large must a planet be?

I met Brown soon after he discovered Eris. If Eris, Makemake, and Haumea became planets, Brown would go down as the greatest planet discoverer of all time. I asked him: "Surely you want them all to be planets along with Pluto, right?"

Eris (the maybe planet)

Wrong.

From the beginning, Brown doubted that Eris was a planet. "Right away I told my wife that Eris, like Pluto, isn't a planet," Brown said. "She responded, 'Not a planet? Don't be an idiot!'" Even Brown's daughter couldn't agree. She loved Pluto and wanted it to stay a planet. The Pluto debate raged in his own house!

Brown did not think he was a "discoverer of planets." "Look," he told me, "I didn't find anything big and important in the solar system. I didn't find Uranus or Neptune. What I did was cool, but let's put this in perspective."

Don't be so humble!

Yeah, you discovered new planets!

Mike Brown's wife and daughter

# Pluto: Not a Planet in New York

The other person partially responsible for the great Pluto debate is Neil deGrasse Tyson, an American astrophysicist and director of the Hayden Planetarium in New York City. In 2000, his planetarium redesigned an exhibit on the solar system. That exhibit did not include Pluto as a planet. Tyson publicly proclaimed that there are really only eight planets in the solar system and Pluto is not one of them!

Lots of people thought this outrageous. Kicking Pluto out of the planet club! How dare he do that to Pluto! At first, Tyson received hate mail from kids and grown-ups for his decision to demote Pluto. They wrote letters that started out

Neil deGrasse Tyson

# PLUTO FAN CLUB

Dear Scientist,

I just learned that Pluto isn't a planet anymore. Why did you do that? Pluto is a really cool place and I don't think it would like not being a planet. It is my favorite planet and now I don't have a favorite planet anymore.

Please write back and please let me know what Pluto ever did to you.

"Dear Mr. Tyson" or "Dear Scientist." And they asked tough questions:

"Why do you think Pluto is no longer a planet?"

"Do people live on Pluto? And if so, don't you think they are sad to not live on a planet anymore?"

"Why can't Pluto stay a planet?"

And they gave some good reasons to keep Pluto as a planet:

"You are going to have to take all the books away and change them."

"But Pluto has moons. Planets have moons. Doesn't that mean that it should be a planet?"

"If it's small, that doesn't mean it doesn't have to be a planet."

"Pluto is my favorite planet and now I don't have a favorite planet anymore."

I'll be honest, I was a little upset about this too. I mean, who did Tyson think he was? He just made up his mind that

Pluto wasn't a planet anymore—all on his own. We need to get together and discuss these things first before making rash decisions. We need to work together as a community of scientists.

Some other astronomers decided to fight back and said if Tyson could downgrade Pluto, then they would downgrade his planetarium to a movie theater. That may not sound like a big deal, but among scientists that is the ultimate insult!

But as time went on, students (and I too) thought more about the subject. Their letters to Tyson changed and became nicer. One kid even wrote how wrong it was for all the other

kids to write nasty letters to him. He apologized for those kids. "We're sorry about giving you mean letters saying we love Pluto but not you. I'm very sorry. It'll be okay."

Another kid wrote that change like this was just a part of science. "We just have to get over it," he wrote. And, "Science will make you smart."

In the end, the combined work of Tyson and Brown changed how we'd look at Pluto forever. Tyson got people debating about what should and shouldn't be a planet (and took a lot of the hate mail). And Brown found so many Pluto-like objects that it made everything a lot more complicated. Now, scientists and people all around the world were unsure. Action was needed to answer the question "What is a planet?"

# So, What Is a Planet?

Okay, we've thrown a lot of facts and history around and your grown-ups may be getting confused. But that's okay. You still have their attention and they may want to hear from experts next. The International Astronomical Union (IAU) is the only group that can name objects in space as well as features on those objects. You can't just name a star or a crater on the Moon. You can't call things "My Dog Spike" or "Fluffy" or "Mommy." There are rules for this stuff. You have to get approval from the IAU. Their membership is made up of the most prestigious and experienced astronomers in the world. Every three years, they meet to talk about space.

In 2006, IAU leaders understood that it was time to tackle the Pluto debate.

IAU superheroes

The nine planets at that time were big round things that went around the Sun. That's it. But so many astronomers were arguing with one another that the IAU decided it was the moment to get serious and really define a planet.

The IAU decided that a planet is an object that

**1. IS IN ORBIT AROUND THE SUN;**

**2. HAS SUFFICIENT MASS FOR ITS SELF-GRAVITY TO OVERCOME RIGID BODY FORCES SO THAT IT ASSUMES A HYDROSTATIC EQUILIBRIUM (NEARLY ROUND) SHAPE; AND**

**3. HAS CLEARED THE NEIGHBORHOOD AROUND ITS ORBIT.**

If you think that definition is confusing, you are not alone! After all, astronomers have to be much better at science and math than English and writing. However, let's make sense of it.

Part 1 is simple enough. A planet must orbit the Sun. Okay, pretty much everything in the solar system, including planets, asteroids, and comets, circles the Sun. So that part of the definition covers a lot, including Pluto. Your grown-ups may look pretty triumphant at this point.

Part 2 totally sounds like gibberish. Even I think the astronomers made it way too complicated. But all it really means is that a planet must be large enough to be round. Most round objects in space are big enough to have enough gravity and time to become round. And there is no doubt that a round object just looks more planet-y. Other than planets, astronomers knew of only five other round things going around the Sun: four Kuiper Belt objects (including Pluto) and one asteroid (Ceres). Everything else was not round. So after part 2, Pluto is still a planet. (At this point in the proceedings, your grown-ups are probably lulled into a false sense of security. They have been right all along!)

But part 3 is the important one. This is the rule that made Pluto not a planet. A planet has to have "cleared the neighborhood around its orbit." What the heck does that mean?

49

The astronomers meant that a planet dominates its area. It's the boss of its orbit. Remember all those other objects that astronomers discovered out beyond Neptune's orbit? Eris, Haumea, Makemake, and thousands of other small, icy objects circle the Sun from great distances along with Pluto. In that region of the solar system, one dominant "planet" is the boss, and it is not Pluto. It's Neptune! Neptune is by far the mover and shaker of the outer solar system and is responsible for

OUTTA MY WAY!

putting Pluto on its long, looping path around the Sun. Neptune is the planet in the area and cannot share that title with another lesser object.

This part of the definition also forbids any asteroids from being planets (even the round ones). Asteroids are not planets because there are so many of them (more than 700,000) sharing a similar space (mainly between the orbits of Mars and Jupiter). Ceres is the largest asteroid, and although it *is* big enough to be round, it *is not* massive enough to carve out a unique spot in the asteroid belt. Because no one asteroid dominates its space in the solar system, none of them are full-fledged planets.

# What Astronomers Meant to Say

Your grown-ups may still be confused. Let's make this simpler. A planet is "a big, uniquely dominant thing that orbits a star." Or even shorter: "A planet is a boss." Mercury is the biggest, most important thing in its region of space—as are Venus, Earth, Mars, Jupiter, Saturn, Uranus, and Neptune. Each has no rival other than the Sun. This is not true for any other object in the solar system. That part and that part alone makes them unique.

Ceres shares its orbit with more than 700,000 similar objects that circle the Sun between Mars and Jupiter. Those are asteroids. Pluto shares its orbit with lots and lots of similar things far from the Sun. Those are plutoids (the nickname for KBOs).

Some moons are really large and important, but they circle something other than a star (the Sun), so they don't count as planets. Those are moons.

That leaves us with eight special objects in our solar system, second in importance only to the Sun. Those are the planets!

# SPACE OBJECT CLASSIFICATION GUIDE!

You discovered an object in the solar system: Congratulations! Now you'll need to identify what type of object it is. Start by answering the questions and following the instructions below.

**Question 1:** Does it orbit the Sun? (If yes, go to Question 2. If no, go to the Moon Question 1.)

**Question 2:** Is it big enough to be round? (If yes, go to Question 3. If no, it is an asteroid, comet, KBO, or other minor planet.)

**Question 3:** Does it absolutely dominate its place in space? (If yes, it is a planet. If no, it is a dwarf planet.)

ROUND          NOT ROUND

**Moon Question 1:** Does it circle around a planet, dwarf planet, asteroid, or KBO? (If yes, it is a moon. If no, it just might be a satellite or a UFO: unidentified flying object.)

# What Is Pluto, Then?

The IAU was *not* done yet. Before they went home to their observatories, they adopted two other categories: dwarf planets and small solar system bodies.

They defined a dwarf planet as a celestial body that:

**1. IS IN ORBIT AROUND THE SUN;**

**2. HAS SUFFICIENT MASS FOR ITS SELF-GRAVITY TO OVERCOME RIGID BODY FORCES SO THAT IT ASSUMES A HYDROSTATIC EQUILIBRIUM (NEARLY ROUND) SHAPE;**

**3. HAS NOT CLEARED THE NEIGHBORHOOD AROUND ITS ORBIT; AND**

**4. IS NOT A SATELLITE.**

So a dwarf planet must go around the Sun, be round, not dominate its region of space, and not be a satellite (a fancy word for a moon). So Pluto is now a KBO and a dwarf planet. There are currently five recognized dwarf planets. Four of them are far from the Sun: Pluto, Eris, Haumea, and

Makemake. And one of them is closer to the Sun: Ceres. Yes, Ceres is an asteroid and a dwarf planet. Why? Because it's roundish! (Those round planet-lovers are persuasive.)

The members of the IAU approved this definition for the last category:

## ALL OTHER OBJECTS, EXCEPT SATELLITES, ORBITING THE SUN SHALL BE REFERRED TO COLLECTIVELY AS "SMALL SOLAR SYSTEM BODIES."

Wow, that was a much shorter definition. And that certainly takes care of everything else. I imagine that the astronomers were getting tired by this point and wanted to get home, have a snack, and take a nap.

But asteroids, small KBOs, comets, rocks, pebbles, ice, and dust were all to be considered small solar system bodies. Now, everything in the solar system (other than the Sun) is either a planet, a dwarf planet, a small solar system body, or a moon. The definitions may be clunky and confusing, but they do include everything.

So to sum up the answer to the big planet debate, most astronomers agree:

## A PLANET IS A BIG IMPORTANT THING THAT GOES AROUND A STAR.

Is Pluto big and important? No. But it's still really cool!

# FAST FACTS ABOUT PLUTO

Diameter: 1,476 miles (2,375 km). That's about the distance from Washington, D.C., to Denver, Colorado.

Average distance from the Sun: 3.7 billion miles (5.9 billion km)

Discovered: February 18, 1930

Classification: Dwarf planet

Color: White with light blue, yellow, and brown

Moons: 5 (Charon, Nix, Hydra, Styx, and Kerberos)

A Pluto day (the time it takes for Pluto to spin one time): 6.4 Earth days

A Pluto year (the time it takes for Pluto to circle the Sun one time): 248 Earth years

# Postcard From Pluto

So what if Pluto isn't a planet? It's still an unbelievably cool world! Astronomers couldn't tell much about Pluto from Earth. Even using the best telescopes, the view of this tiny world three billion miles (4.8 billion km) away was small and blurry.

Hey all—
Well, after a
Loooooooong
journey, I finally
made it to PLUTO!
Freezing—but
beautiful. Wish
you were here!
♡ NH

NASA

EARTH

What if they went in for a closer look?

Only a few months before the IAU demoted Pluto, NASA launched a robotic spacecraft called New Horizons to fly by Pluto and examine it up close. New Horizons was the fastest spacecraft launched from Earth, leaving the planet at more than 36,000 miles per hour (58,000 km/h). Even so, it still took 9.5 years to travel to Pluto.

New Horizons spacecraft

After an epic journey, New Horizons flew within 7,800 miles (12,550 km) of Pluto. It sent back some incredible images and remarkable detail of its icy surface. The first thing astronomers noticed was a huge feature on the side of Pluto. Some people think it looks like a heart, a whale's tail, or even the face of Disney's dog Pluto. This bright area of ice is now named Tombaugh Regio after the discoverer of Pluto, Clyde Tombaugh.

Pluto has several craggy, snowcapped mountains. Some of the mountains could be cryovolcanoes. Cryovolcanoes

New Horizons flying by Pluto and its moon Charon

## FAST FACT

On an average day on Pluto, the temperature is between minus 375°F and minus 400°F (−226°C to −240°C).

shoot out liquids and ices made of water, methane, ammonia, and chlorine instead of lava. The material then builds mountains of ice.

Although the surface of Pluto is covered in ice, it's not all frozen solid. It has slow-moving glaciers made of nitrogen ice. These glaciers have carved huge grooves on the surface and left islands of ice behind. Pluto has a glacier called Sputnik Planitia that is about 600 miles (966 km) wide. It may be the biggest glacier in the solar system. And some scientists see evidence that Pluto may have an ocean of water just below the mostly frozen surface.

Pluto may be small and far from the Sun, but it still has an atmosphere. Now, it is nothing like Earth and you couldn't breathe there, but it does give the sky an interesting color. If you were standing on the surface of Pluto, the sky would be blue!

Pluto is a wild, wonderful world, and it just doesn't matter if it's not actually a planet.

# What to Do If Your Grown-ups Fight Back

Okay, so now we're right up to date, and the history part of the lesson is over. Do your grown-ups need a rest? If so, feel free to give them some time. And you might need to prepare yourself, too, as they may throw some tricky questions your way. I'll prepare you with a great answer for anything even the craftiest grown-ups might devise.

## But What If Pluto Was a Planet? Would That Be So Bad?

You need to be prepared for this question from your grown-ups. And your reply could be: "Okay, so if Pluto was a planet, what *else* would be a planet? How many of the plutoids and asteroids and other roundish things in the solar system would be planets?"

    Astronomers actually asked one another that same question. But by letting Pluto stay a planet, you'd have to

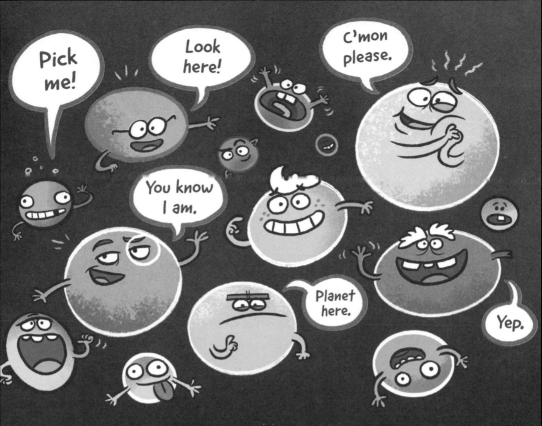

wonder about Eris. Shouldn't it be a planet too? And what about Ceres, and Vesta, and Makemake, and Haumea, and Juno, and Ixion, and Varuna, and Quaoar, and (225088) 2007 OR10, and (307261) 2002 MS4? You couldn't leave them out or they'd be sadder than Pluto!

Where does it stop? Thousands of things could end up being planets. This might actually be your best argument—because who wants to learn the names of 3,000 planets? Even a catchy mnemonic saying would take all day to recite!

# But It's Not Like Earth and Jupiter Have Much in Common!

Yes, some of the smartest grown-ups may make this argument. They could say, "Jupiter is like 1,000 times bigger than Earth and is mostly made of hydrogen gas— while Earth is tiny in comparison and mostly made of rock. How can *they* both be planets?" And these are valid questions, so feel free to congratulate your grown-ups. They are smarter than they look.

Tell them they are correct to question this. It's true that if you put Earth and Jupiter next to each other, they seem to have little in common other than they are both round. Earth is only about 8,000 miles (12,875 km) across, while Jupiter is about 88,000 miles (141,620 km) across.

Hi little rocky guy.

Peeyoo, you're gassy!

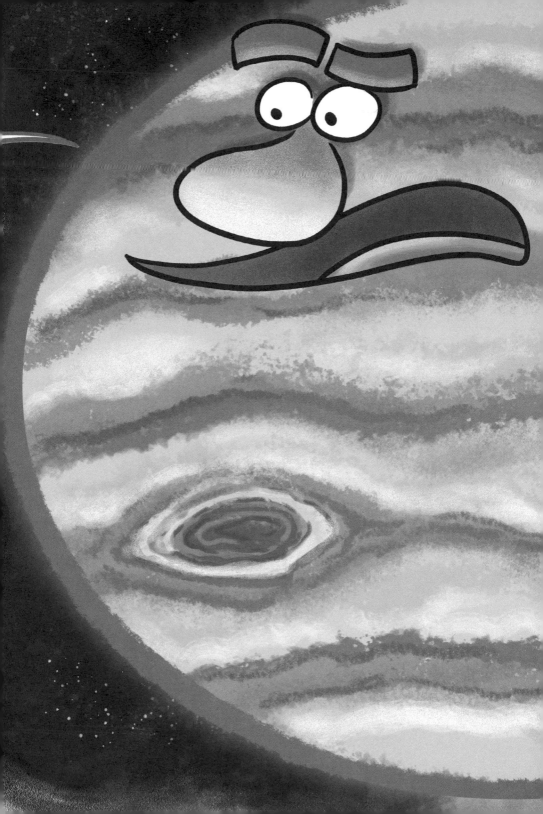

But remember, size does *not* matter. The question is: Are they the biggest, most important things in their place in space? And the answer is yes.

What a planet is *made of* does have some relevance, even though it's not part of the official definition. Instead, it gives us clues about how the planets were formed in the first place. Four planets in our solar system are mostly made of rocks: Mercury, Venus, Earth, and Mars. Four planets in our solar system are mainly gases: Jupiter, Saturn, Uranus, and Neptune.

So you and your grown-ups can make the valid claim that we can break down the category of planets into terrestrial planets that are mostly made of rock and closer to the Sun (Mercury, Venus, Earth, and Mars) and gaseous planets that are mostly made of hydrogen gas and farther from the Sun (Jupiter, Saturn, Uranus, and Neptune). Or, to simplify it, rocky and gassy planets.

Pluto is different. It is not mostly made of rock or gas. By volume, Pluto is mostly ice. If Pluto ever got too close to the Sun, it would melt into a giant puddle of water. This makes Pluto different from the eight planets.

Chill guys.

Gas giants: Jupiter, Saturn, Uranus, Neptune

## FAST FACT

Jupiter is so big that you could fit 1,300 Earths inside it. Its main storm, the Great Red Spot, is larger than our whole planet!

It tells astronomers that Pluto was made from different stuff in the solar system and in a different way than the planets.

"If Earth is a rocky planet and Jupiter is a gassy planet, then c'mon, why can't Pluto just be called an icy planet?" At this point, it is okay to allow your grown-ups to refer to Pluto as an icy planet. It may make them feel better for now. You can pretend you approve by saying, "Hey, that's a good idea. Pluto is really different from the others and should have its own category. Good job!"

Nix

# But Pluto Has Moons!

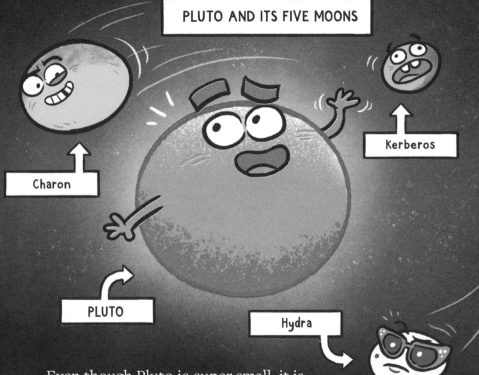

Styx

And another thing! (Your grown-ups might say.)
You're forgetting about moons! Earth has a moon and
it's a planet. Neptune has 14 moons and it's a planet. Jupiter
has 79 moons and it's a planet. Pluto has five moons, but it's
not a planet? What gives?

## PLUTO AND ITS FIVE MOONS

Charon

Kerberos

PLUTO

Hydra

Even though Pluto is super small, it is
still large enough to have five moons circling it.
Charon, by far Pluto's largest moon, is about half the size of

Pluto and they actually go around each other. In fact, one side of Pluto faces one side of Charon all the time. So if you lived on certain parts of Pluto, you would never know Charon existed—you'd be facing the other way!

That's definitely weird, but moons do not make a planet. Mercury and Venus have no moons and they *are* planets.

Dwarf planets Eris, Makemake, and Haumea have moons. Several dozen sweet little asteroids in the asteroid belt have moons as well. An asteroid named Ida keeps a tiny, one-mile (1.6-km)-wide moon in orbit around it named Dactyl.

Astronomers have found lots of objects that have moons in our solar system and they can't all be planets.

Hey Charon, quit mooning me!

# MOONS
## in the
# SOLAR SYSTEM

A moon is an object that goes around a larger object like a planet. Here is the latest moon count for planets and also for other objects in the solar system.

PLANETS

0
Mercury

Venus

1
Earth

0

2
Mars

80
Jupiter

Saturn

Uranus

27

82

14

Neptune

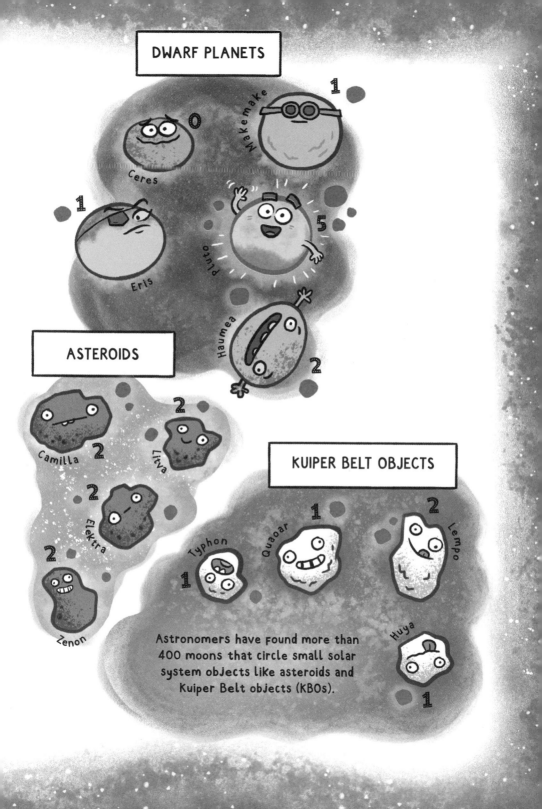

# Nature of Science

When you talk with some adults, they really respect history. When people argue, they sometimes like to see what people in the past did. This is called precedence.

"What's a planet?" is a question that astronomers have been debating for thousands of years.

As we made more discoveries and learned more about our solar system, that definition has changed—a lot!

Science moves forward by collecting observations, information, and evidence. Then, scientists around the world look at this evidence and try to make sense of it. Other scientists review it to make sure it sounds good. Sometimes they debate. Sometimes they argue. In the end, each step brings us a little closer to understanding. It's not perfect, but astronomers try to keep an open mind and to update their ideas. That is the nature of science.

Pluto was not the first planet to be demoted. It may not be the last. Every day, astronomers find a new asteroid. Every week, they identify new stars. Every month, they spot new galaxies.

Astronomers are forever curious, forever exploring. They are constantly scanning the sky to find faint, distant objects in the hopes of locating another planet.

Hubble Space Telescope

Some grown-ups think science is set in stone, that astronomy is just a set of unchangeable facts and laws. Not even! Science is a living, breathing, changing adventure. That's what makes science so fun!

# NUMBER OF PLANETS THROUGHOUT HISTORY

How many planets are there?
Depends on when you ask!

PLANETS

Before 1543: 7 Planets
(Sun, Moon, Mercury, Venus,
Mars, Jupiter, Saturn)

1543: 6 Planets
(Mercury, Venus, Earth,
Mars, Jupiter, Saturn)

1781: 7 Planets
(Mercury, Venus, Earth, Mars,
Jupiter, Saturn, Uranus)

1807: 11 Planets (Mercury, Venus, Earth, Mars,
Ceres, Pallas, Juno, Vesta, Jupiter, Saturn, Uranus)

**1847:** 18 Planets (Mercury, Venus, Earth, Mars, Ceres, Pallas, Juno, Vesta, Astraea, Hebe, Iris, Flora, Metis, Hygiea, Jupiter, Saturn, Uranus, Neptune)

**1860:** 8 Planets (Mercury, Venus, Earth, Mars, Jupiter, Saturn, Uranus, Neptune)

**1930:** 9 Planets (Mercury, Venus, Earth, Mars, Jupiter, Saturn, Uranus, Neptune, Pluto)

**2006:** 8 Planets (Mercury, Venus, Earth, Mars, Jupiter, Saturn, Uranus, Neptune)

TIME

# Introducing... Sedna

Now THAT'S eccentric!

If after all this explanation your grown-ups are feeling sad and missing Pluto, here's a treat you can give them. There's a new oddball to fall in love with. Your grown-ups will love it!

In 2003, astronomers discovered a solar system object they named Sedna. It is almost as big as Pluto but much, much farther away.

Right now, Sedna is twice as far from the Sun as Pluto. And remember how Pluto's path around the Sun was elliptical (or looked like an oval)? Sedna's orbit is even wilder. Its path is so long, crazy, and stretched out that Sedna will eventually travel to a distance about 84 billion miles (135 billion km) away.

# FAST FACTS ABOUT SEDNA

Diameter: Between 800 and 1,100 miles
(1,290 and 1,770 km)

Distance from
the Sun:
7 billion miles at closest
(11 billion km)
to 84 billion miles
at furthest
(135 billion km)

Classification:
Small solar
system body

Moons: 0
(so far)

Color:
Red

Discovered:
November 14, 2003

A Sedna day
(the time it takes
for Sedna to spin
one time):
10 Earth hours

A Sedna year (the time it takes for Sedna to
circle the Sun one time): 10,500 Earth years

That's about 19 times farther than the farthest Pluto ever gets from the Sun. In fact, Sedna goes so far away that it takes about 10,500 years to circle the Sun one time!

Sedna is also one of the reddest objects in space (about as red as the planet Mars). While Mars's color comes from rust on its surface, Sedna's color comes from this slushy stuff on its surface called tholins. After sunlight shines on tholins, even ones that are so far from the Sun, they turn red.

Sedna is a one-of-a-kind object. Astronomers aren't even sure what to call it. It's in the Kuiper Belt, but it also goes farther away into the region of the comets called the Oort Cloud. Is it round enough to be a dwarf planet? We're not sure. Does it have a moon? No moons have been found yet.

So Sedna is cuter than Pluto, farther than Pluto, more colorful than Pluto, and is super mysterious. If your grown-ups liked Pluto because it was unique, they will absolutely *love* Sedna. In fact, tell them, "Sedna is the new Pluto." We should make T-shirts.

# Planet Nine

Some astronomers believe that Sedna's weirdness is a clue to a hidden world. Its path around the Sun is so strange that perhaps another planet at the edge of the solar system makes it behave in that way. Astronomer Mike Brown (yes, the same Mike Brown who found Eris, Sedna, and more) is searching for it. He has given it a name: Planet Nine.

Is it weird to give a name to a planet no one has ever seen and may not actually exist?

Mike Brown

PLANET NINE?

Brown worked with fellow astronomer Konstantin Batygin to figure out mathematically why Sedna behaves so strangely. On paper, if there existed an object the size of Neptune that was very dark and very far away, it could explain Sedna's behavior.

If this sounds a lot like how Le Verrier and Adams found Neptune, you're right. But this time, the discovery is not so easy. Planet Nine may be so dark and so far that it will take a new, giant telescope to discover it—a telescope and camera no one has built yet. And then again, Planet Nine may not even exist.

But imagine if astronomers find another big object, bigger than Earth, bigger than Neptune, that goes around the Sun. That would be exciting! We'd get to debate what is a planet again!

# The New and Improved Solar System

Just days after the demotion of Pluto, I taught a class of eight- and nine-year-olds about planets. After my presentation, one of the students cautiously approached me to break the news about Pluto. She said, "You know, Mr. Dean, Pluto is no longer a planet."

I replied that I had heard that.

She went on to reassure me: "It's a dwarf planet and it's okay. That's where it belongs, with all its other brothers and sisters out there."

I thanked her for her concern. It actually did make me feel better.

She was right. Science marches on. New discoveries are opening our eyes to what is out there. Change is exciting!

Now we can embrace a new saying to remember the order of the eight planets: My Very Educated Mother Just Served Us *Nachos*.

Of course, it's possible that the definition of a planet may change again. And that's okay. Whatever the official definition of *planet*, it should be simple. In the past, you knew what a planet was when you saw it. It still can be that way. I say if we ever have another great planet debate, we should not leave it to astronomers alone. We should give this assignment to people like you. Put 11 young people in a room with the information on the largest objects in the solar system, provide cookies and drinks, nachos and pizza, and by the end of the day they will create a definition of a planet—and be able to explain it. I trust their judgment and would be honored to share the latest definition of *planet* with everyone.

# Time Line of Discovery

Now that you know the twists and turns in the story of how we understand the solar system, take a look below for a recap. These are the moments when astronomers discovered a new planet (or what they thought was a new planet).

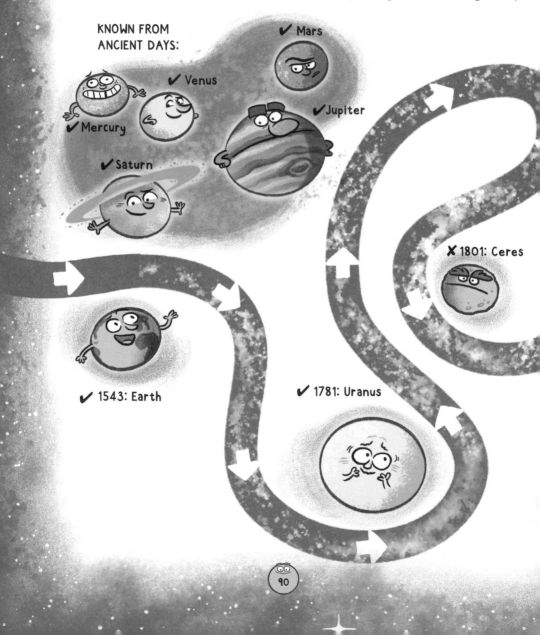

KNOWN FROM ANCIENT DAYS:

✔ Mars

✔ Venus

✔ Mercury

✔ Jupiter

✔ Saturn

✗ 1801: Ceres

✔ 1543: Earth

✔ 1781: Uranus

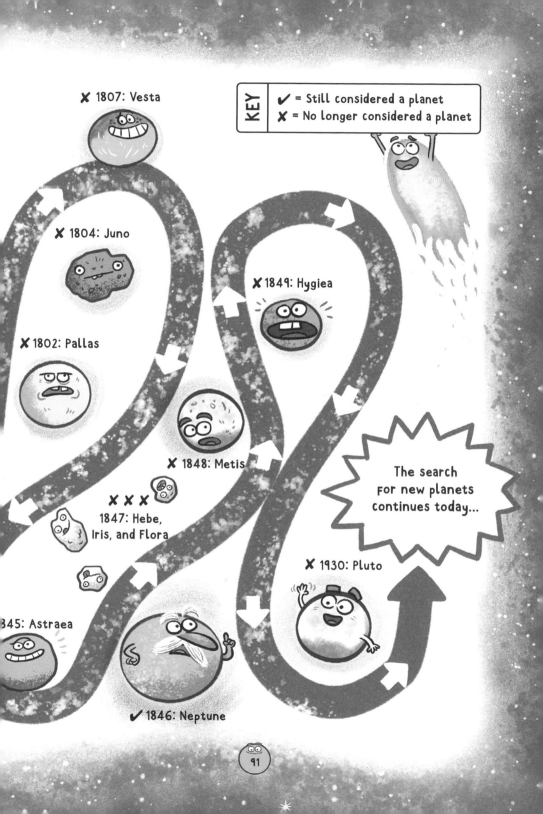

# What Type of Solar System Object Are You?

I like to give objects in the solar system a little personality. I know they're just lifeless chunks of rock, ice, dust, and gas, but it's sometimes fun to look for yourself in the heavens above. The questions below could help you figure out what planetary object you are most like—moon, asteroid, planet, or dwarf planet. Test your friends and especially your grown-ups. Maybe you will find out that you know some plutoids!

1. **What type of matter do you prefer?**

   a) Ice
   b) Air
   c) Dirt
   d) Rock

2. **What do you think is the most exciting type of weather?**

   a) Cold and snowy
   b) Windy
   c) All types
   d) Drastically changing every day

3. **Which house is the most appealing?**

   a) Ice palace
   b) House in the clouds
   c) Big cabin by the mountains
   d) Small shack with a view of town

4. **Which do you find most funny?**

   a) Someone sliding around on ice
   b) Someone farting
   c) Someone doing a belly flop into the water
   d) Someone juggling rocks

5. **How do people describe you?**

   a) You are "far out."
   b) You are "the boss."
   c) You are "down to earth."
   d) You are "always running around."

Woohoo! Which are you?

If you answered **a** to most
of these questions, you are a
dwarf planet like Pluto.

If you mainly answered **b**,
you are a gas giant planet
like Jupiter.

If you answered **c** a
lot, you are a terrestrial
planet like Earth.

If you answered **d** most
frequently, you are an
asteroid or moon.

What other questions could you ask to find out what kind
of solar system object you are?

# Test Your Grown-ups!

Now you can test your grown-ups to see what you taught them
(and how much they paid attention).

1. **Young astronomer Clyde Tombaugh discovered Pluto in 1930. He found it by studying:**

   a) Textbooks
   b) Photographs
   c) Rocks
   d) His feet

2. **Pluto was named by an 11-year-old called:**

   a) Venetia Burney
   b) Valerie Blake
   c) Venus Brown
   d) Veronica Bleeker

3. **How many moons does Pluto have?**

   a) 0
   b) 1
   c) 5
   d) 1,359

4. **What is Pluto?**

   a) A dwarf planet
   b) A Kuiper Belt object
   c) An object that used to be a planet
   d) All of the above

5. **Pluto is mostly made of...**

   a) Ice
   b) Orange juice
   c) Salt
   d) Cheese

6. **Pluto's sky is...**

   a) Red
   b) Blue
   c) Yellow
   d) Polka dot

7. **What was the name of the spacecraft that flew past Pluto?**

   a) Zeus Express
   b) Styx Crossing
   c) Charon Osbourne
   d) New Horizons

8. **Pluto's orbit is in the shape of:**

   a) An ellipse
   b) A circle
   c) A triangle
   d) A diamond

WHOOSH!

**9.** Another cool and strange object in the solar system is called:

a) Sedna
b) Sidney
c) Sidcup
d) Simples

**10.** How many Plutos could you fit inside Earth?

a) 3.5
b) 16
c) 170
d) 6,000

**11.** How many years does it take for Pluto to go around the Sun?

a) 12
b) 248
c) 555
d) 10,004

**12.** What's the name of the dwarf planet almost exactly the same size as Pluto?

a) Vesta
b) Neptune
c) Rover
d) Eris

**13.** What is the name of the object astronomers are searching for in the outer solar system?

a) Planet Nine
b) Triton Four
c) Pluto Two
d) Seven Eleven

**14.** Pluto is not a planet anymore because...

a) It's too small
b) It's not round
c) It shares its space with too many other similar things
d) It's too far away from the Sun

**15.** In what year was Pluto declared NOT a planet?

a) 1906
b) 1966
c) 2006
d) Never. It's still a planet*

*If this is your grown-up's answer, I'm afraid it's an immediate fail.

Answers: 1: b; 2: a; 3: c; 4: d; 5: a; 6: b; 7: d; 8: a; 9: a; 10: c; 11: b; 12: d; 13: a; 14: c; 15: c

# Sources

## BOOKS

Brown, Mike. *How I Killed Pluto and Why It Had It Coming*. Random House, 2012.

Consolmagno, Guy, and Dan M. Davis. *Turn Left at Orion*. Cambridge University Press, 2000.

Dickinson, Terence. *Nightwatch*. Firefly Books, 1998.

Regas, Dean. 100 *Things to See in the Night Sky, Expanded Edition*. Adams Media, 2020.

Regas, Dean. *Facts From Space!* Adams Media, 2016.

Stern, Alan. *Chasing New Horizons: Inside the Epic First Mission to Pluto*. Picador, 2018.

Tyson, Neil deGrasse. *The Pluto Files: The Rise and Fall of America's Favorite Planet*. W. W. Norton & Company, 2014.

## WEBSITES

Gas Giants, Facts About the Outer Planets: space.com/30372-gas-giants.html

Hubble Site, Hubble Space Telescope: hubblesite.org

NASA Science, Solar System Exploration, Planets of Our Solar System: solarsystem.nasa.gov/planets/overview

NASA Science, Pluto: solarsystem.nasa.gov/planets/dwarf-planets/pluto/overview

NASA Science, Kuiper Belt: solarsystem.nasa.gov/solar-system/kuiper-belt/overview

NASA Science, Asteroids, Comets, and Meteors: solarsystem.nasa.gov/asteroids-comets-and-meteors/overview

NASA New Horizons: nasa.gov/mission_pages/newhorizons/main/index.html

New Horizons, NASA's Mission to Pluto and the Kuiper Belt: pluto.jhuapl.edu

The Nine Planets: nineplanets.org

The Planets: theplanets.org

Terrestrial Planets, Definition and Facts About the Inner Planets: space.com/17028-terrestrial-planets.html

# Index

· · · · · ·

**Boldface indicates illustrations.**

# Glossary

**Definitions of terms in this book—and some extras, in case you need them for teaching your grown-ups about space.**

**ASTEROID**—A small rocky object that orbits the Sun.

**ASTEROID BELT**—The region in the solar system, between the orbits of Mars and Jupiter, where most asteroids circle the Sun.

**ASTRONOMER**—A person who is an expert in astronomy and makes observations of and studies the universe.

**ASTRONOMICAL UNIT** (often abbreviated AU)—A unit of measurement that is the average distance between Earth and the Sun—1 AU is equal to 92,955,807 miles (149,597,870 km).

**ASTRONOMY**—The field of science that studies objects in space and everything in the universe.

**ATMOSPHERE**—The gases surrounding a planet, star, or satellite.

**COMET**—A body of rock, dust, and ice that orbits the Sun in an elongated orbit. When it is near the Sun, a comet shoots off gases that form a long streaming tail.

**CONSTELLATION**—A group of stars that form a recognizable pattern. Many constellations take the form of animals, mythological people and creatures, and scientific instruments.

**CORONA**—The outermost layer of gases in the Sun's atmosphere.

**COSMOLOGY**—The study of the beginning, end, and structure of the whole universe.

**CRATER**—A circular depression in the surface of a planet, moon, or other object in space caused by a meteorite impact or by volcanic action.

**DENSITY**—A measurement of how much mass an object has within a certain amount of space.

**DIAMETER**—The distance through the center of an object or shape from one side to the other; an object's width.

**DWARF PLANET**—An object that goes around the Sun and is nearly spherical in shape but has not cleared its orbit like a planet does. Pluto, Eris, Makemake, Haumea, and Ceres are examples of dwarf planets.

**ELLIPSE**—An oval shape; the shape of every planetary orbit in our solar system.

**EXOPLANET**—A planet that orbits a star other than the Sun.

**GALAXY**—An extremely large grouping of stars, gas, and dust bound together by gravity.

**GAS GIANT PLANET**—A large planet made mostly of gases such as hydrogen and helium. In our solar system, Jupiter, Saturn, Uranus, and Neptune are gas giants.

**GEOCENTRIC MODEL**—A theory that maps out the solar system with Earth in the center.

**GRAVITY**—The force that pulls objects toward each other. Everything with mass has gravity.

**HABITABLE ZONE** (also called the "Goldilocks Zone")—The region around a star in which a planet could have liquid water and possibly support life.

**HELIOCENTRIC MODEL**—A theory that maps the solar system with the Sun in the center.

**INTERSTELLAR**—Existing or traveling between the stars.

**KUIPER BELT**—The region of the solar system beyond the orbit of Neptune where dwarf planets, comets, and other small objects circle the Sun.

**LIGHT-YEAR**—The distance light travels in a year: 5.88 trillion miles (9.46 trillion km).

**MASS**—The total quantity of material in an object, determining its gravity and resistance to movement.

**METEOR**—An object that falls from space and heats up in Earth's atmosphere; a "shooting star."

**METEORITE**—An object that falls from space, survives its fiery plunge through the atmosphere, and crashes to Earth.

**METEOROID**—A smaller asteroid.

**MOON**—An object in space that circles a planet, dwarf planet, or asteroid.

**NEAR-EARTH OBJECT**—An asteroid or comet whose orbit brings it close to Earth.

**OBSERVATORY**—A building with instruments for studying the sky, including telescopes.

**OORT CLOUD**—A region of the solar system beyond the Kuiper Belt that is the source of long-period comets that take hundreds of years to orbit the Sun.

**ORBIT**—The regular path an object in space follows as it revolves around another body.

**PLANET**—A nearly spherical object that circles the Sun and has cleared its orbit of similar-sized objects.

**PLANET X**—The nickname of a planet believed to exist somewhere in the solar system beyond Neptune's orbit that has not yet been discovered.

**PLANETARIUM**—A room in which stars and constellations are projected onto a ceiling or dome.

**PLUTOID**—An object similar to and including Pluto that orbits the Sun farther than Neptune and is big enough to be nearly round.

**REVOLVE**—To move completely around another object; to orbit.

**ROTATE**—To spin around like a top.

**SATELLITE**—A natural or human-made object that revolves around a planet.

**SMALL SOLAR SYSTEM BODIES**—Objects that go around the Sun that are not planets, dwarf planets, moons, or satellites.

**STAR**—An object in space that fuses elements to create its own light and heat.

**TERRESTRIAL PLANET**—A planet made mostly of rocks. In our solar system, Mercury, Venus, Earth, and Mars are terrestrial planets.

# Meet the Author

Dean Regas has been the astronomer for the Cincinnati Observatory since 2000. He is a renowned educator, author, national popularizer of astronomy, and expert in observational astronomy.

An extremely engaging and media-savvy astronomy lecturer, he has served as the observatory's outreach astronomer since 2000, and as one of NASA's solar system ambassadors, responsible for sharing its latest science and discoveries.

From 2010 to 2019, Dean was the cohost of the PBS program *Star Gazers*. He is the author of four books, including *Facts from Space*, *100 Things to See in the Night Sky*, and *100 Things to See in the Southern Night Sky* (all Adams Media), and *National Geographic Kids 1,000 Facts About Space*.

Dean is a contributing editor to *Sky and Telescope* magazine and a contributor to *Astronomy* magazine, where he won the 2008 Out-of-this-World Award for astronomy education. Dean has written more than 150 astronomy articles for the *Cincinnati Enquirer* and has blogged for the *Huffington Post*. He is regularly featured on television and radio, including as a frequent guest on National Public Radio's *Science Friday* with Ira Flatow and NPR's *Here & Now* with Robin Young. He also hosts an astronomy podcast with Anna Hehman called *Looking Up*.

At the Cincinnati Observatory, he has developed his skills as a dynamic writer and public speaker who brings the complicated field of astronomy down to Earth for students of all ages.

## FAST FACT

In 2015, Dean Regas had a space object named for him—"8815 Deanregas" is a Florian asteroid from a family of stony asteroids.

**BRITANNICA
BOOKS**

Britannica Books is an imprint of What on Earth Publishing,
published in collaboration with Britannica, Inc.
Allington Castle, Maidstone, Kent ME16 0NB, United Kingdom
30 Ridge Road Unit B, Greenbelt, Maryland, 20770, United States

First published in the United States in 2022

Written by Dean Regas
Illustrated by Aaron Blecha
Designed by Cara Llewellyn
Cover design by Andy Forshaw and Nell Wood
Developed by Potomac Global Media: Kevin Mulroy, Publisher; Barbara Brownell Grogan,
Editor in Chief; Jane Sunderland and Heather McElwain, Contributing Editors
Indexed by Timothy Griffin
Book production and print production by Booklabs.co.uk

Encyclopaedia Britannica
Alison Eldridge, Managing Editor; Michele Rita Metych and William Gosner, Fact-Checkers

Britannica Books
Nancy Feresten, Publisher; Natalie Bellos, Executive Editor; Meg Osborne, Assistant Editor;
Andy Forshaw, Art Director; Nell Wood, Junior Designer

Library of Congress Cataloging-in-Publication Data available upon request

ISBN: 9781913750510

Printed in India. RP/Haryana, India/12/2021

1 3 5 7 9 10 8 6 4 2

whatonearthbooks.com
britannica-books.com

MIX
Paper from
responsible sources
FSC® C016779

# Discover more books that are out of this world

A stunning compendium of knowledge, spanning the origins of the Universe to the present day and beyond.

A brilliantly brainy book of lists that will keep kids and their grown-ups absorbed for hours!

A series of fact-filled adventures, where every fact connects to the next in surprising and hilarious ways.

## BRITANNICA BOOKS

britannica-books.com

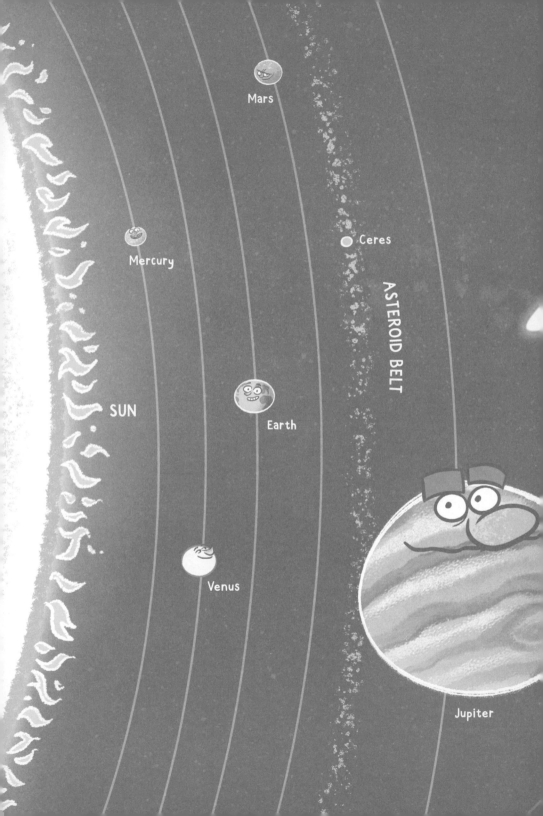